ELNA BRANDIE

PINTEREST MARKETING SUCCESS

The Essential Guide to Pinterest Marketing for Beginners, Discover How You Can Use Pinterest To Effectively Promote Your Products and Business

Descrierea CIP a Bibliotecii Naţionale a României
ELNA BRANDIE
    PINTEREST MARKETING SUCCESS. The Essential
Guide to Pinterest Marketing for Beginners, Discover How You
Can Use Pinterest To Effectively Promote Your Products and
Business / Elna Brandie – Bucharest: Editura My Ebook, 2021
    ISBN

ELNA BRANDIE

PINTEREST MARKETING SUCCESS
The Essential Guide to Pinterest Marketing for Beginners, Discover How You Can Use Pinterest To Effectively Promote Your Products and Business

My Ebook Publishing House
Bucharest, 2021

TABLE OF CONTENTS

INTRODUCTION

If you run your own business and focus your social media marketing efforts only on platforms like Twitter and Facebook, you aren't alone. But that doesn't mean you're in good company. Some of the world's largest brands use Pinterest to market their products and services. Why? It works.

While other social media platforms are becoming more visual, Pinterest got there first and did it best. In a world where we have to grab a new viewer's attention in 7 seconds, Pinterest can do that for you with a minimum of text because you image says so much.

What is Pinterest?

Pinterest is a visual bookmarking tool where people look for and save new and creative ideas. The idea you bookmark is called a pin, and add pins to different boards that you create so all the information you save is organized, so it's easy to find later when you want it. Plus, every pin you post on your Pinterest boards includes a link to the site where it originates from, so you can always go directly to the source to learn more details or to buy products.

Imagine looking through a catalog or an online store. What usually grabs your attention for an item first? The text description? Probably not. It's much more likely the image of the product is what grabs you. After that, you read the text to learn the details. This is the exact premise Pinterest is built on. So you can see, just about any business could utilize Pinterest to grow their brand recognition, gain exposure, improve website traffic, heighten social media engagement and generate more revenue!

If you believe you don't have time to manage one more social media platform, consider these statistics.

- 93% of Pinners use Pinterest for planning purchases.

- 87% of Pinners have purchased something because of Pinterest.

- 72% of Pinners access Pinterest to determine what to buy offline.

- Over 5% of all referral traffic to websites is from Pinterest.

- Millennials use Pinterest just as much as Instagram.

- The median age of Pinners is 40, but the majority of active Pinners are below 40 years old.

- Approximately 50% of Pinners have a yearly income of $50K, while 10% have household incomes of over $125K.

A wide range of age groups are represented on Pinterest, and those Pinners have a nice disposable income. Those same Pinners use Pinterest not only to get ideas, but they go there to make their buying decisions.

Pinterest, more than any other social media platform, can be utilized to improve brand recognition and make sales.

Why You Should Use Pinterest for Business

You may still need more convincing. We get it. Your time is precious, and you may not want to turn it over to compete in yet another social media outlet. To encourage you further, we've outlined some of the best reasons why you should be using Pinterest right here.

- Pinners are open to marketing - Around 2/3 of all pins are from businesses. People actually go to Pinterest to shop. They know they are being "sold to" there and they're good with that...unlike other social media platforms.

- Pinterest is more of a search engine than a social media site.

Pinners use the Smart Feed Algorithm and advanced search technology of Pinterest to guide them to ideas they want to explore. Sure, they share pins too, but they consciously go to Pinterest to explore fresh ideas so they *can* share them.

- A Pin has a shelf-life of 160% longer than on other social media platforms! To be successful on other social media sites, you have to continually put your content out there, so people don't miss it in their feeds. If someone isn't on their profile when you post on most social media, they won't see it. But content on Pinterest is always at their fingertips. Most Pinners use the search feature on a regular basis, which means your content stays evergreen and available.

- Active Pinners have a 9% higher household income than any other social media users. Add to that fact that Pinners use Pinterest to help them make buying decisions and you've got a huge reason for adding Pinterest to your social media marketing!

- Pinners state that they use other sources of media, such as TV, magazines, and catalogs less frequently than the average consumer. What this means to you is that you can utilize the free power of Pinterest to reach sought-after demographics while keeping your marketing budget low.

- The average purchase from a Pinner is $58.95, which is higher than any other social media outlet.

- Pinterest offers popular keywords and trending products in their search bubbles in real time. This means you can use Pinterest to learn about emerging trends in any industry or niche. This gives you the competitive edge. And, using Promoted Pins allows you to track what products are growing in popularity or are losing it so you can improve your business products and services before everyone else.

- Pinterest continues to grow in popularity with different demographic groups, including men.

- The referral traffic from Pinterest is second only to Facebook. Twitter, for example, only refers approximately 1% of all traffic.

With Pinterest's growing popularity, now is the time to get into the game. Another important point for you to know as a business owner looking for marketing mojo - most businesses use Pinterest ineffectively, if not downright wrong. By learning what we have to teach you in this eBook, you will have what you need to use Pinterest the smart and savvy way.

Watch out, competition!

Now that you're convinced let's get started!

PINTEREST BASICS: GETTING STARTED

Although this eBook focuses mostly on smart ways to make a splash with your marketing efforts of Pinterest, it's important to start the way you mean to go on. For example, many business owners who use Pinterest don't use a Business Account. This is a shame because that type of account offers some of the most important features for businesses.

A Pinterest business account offers:

- Rich Pins
- Promoted Pins
- Analytics

All of which we will discuss further later on.

If you enjoy using Pinterest personally, don't worry. You can keep your personal profile and add a business one to it! And, you won't lose anything!

To get started, go to Pinterest and chose:

1. Start a Business Profile

2. Convert your Personal Profile into a Business account.

Your next step is to fill out your profile completely, including most recent headshot or logo. Add a good description of what your company does. Add what you are passionate about and what you love to Pin. This will help Pinners find and connect with you.

Don't forget to include your website address in your profile. You'll need that to verify your site, which you must do to access your Analytics.

To learn more about setting up your Business Account, go here

Next step, verify your website. You can find step-by-step instructions on how to do that here

Once you've verified your site, you can request access to Rich Pins. Now's a good time to do that, so you'll have the ability to do it when you're ready for it.

What are Rich Pins?

Basically, Rich Pins provide more context about your idea because they show the visitor additional information directly on the pin!

Pinterest describes them as:

"Rich Pins are Pins that include extra information right on the Pin itself. Currently, there are four types of Rich Pins: recipe, article, product, and app."

This is a great benefit to businesses because it lays out more of the information people will need to know about your business. Here's a rundown of how Rich Pins can provide outstanding marketing value for your business:

1. Product - you can show the description of the product, price and stock level/status on pins from your website.

2. Recipe - you can show ingredients, cooking time, type of food (sugar-free, paleo, etc.) and servicing size from pins on your site.

3. App Install - you can take iOS users directly to the app store so they can download your app.

4. Articles - you can show the title, headline, description, and author of the article and blog posts on pins from your site.

Rich Pin images also have special features that make them stand out more. The feature makes your pins pop with bolded heading and subheading, a different, more extensive description, link to article and author details. All of these little extras make a big difference to people who are considering clicking on the link. By supplying them with more of the important details, they'll know right away if you have what they are looking for, which offers you a more targeted audience on your site.

Remember that you have to get access to Rich Pins and after that, you have to verify your approval, so it's wise to ask for access as soon as you set up your profile and verify your website. It can take 2 or 3 weeks to get your approval verified, so go ahead and take this step now, so you're ready for anything later. To learn how to set up Rich Pins for your site, go here.

Pin a What?

Before you start using your account, let's cover the Pinterest terminology you'll need to know, so you don't stumble around.

1. Boards

You can think of Boards as bulletin boards you might put up around your house. This is where you post new content that you find interesting, helpful or inspiring (or all three!) Boards are based on categories. For example, you may have a Board called "Low-Carb Desserts." Every low-carb dessert recipe, how-to, etc. would be posted to that board. Boards keep you organized and help people find your content.

2. Secret Boards

These are "bulletin boards" that are private - ideas you want to collect, but don't want to share with your followers. No one can see these posts unless you make them public later.

3. Group Boards

These boards are used by multiple pinners. These are great if you are launching a new product line with another business, for example, or are collaborating on a project.

4. Pin

A Pin is the "post" you add to your boards. The focal point is an image that includes are redirected link to an external webpage, such as a landing page, blog post, video, etc.

5. RePin

Repinning is what someone does when they save one of your Pins to one of their boards. This is the way Pinners share other people's pins with their friends and followers. It's like "Sharing" on Facebook or "Retweeting" on Twitter.

6. Comments and Likes

These are the same as on other social media channels, such as Facebook. You can leave a comment on pins you find interesting, or you can click "like" to show you find the pin helpful or interesting.

7. Pin It Button

This is a widget or plugin you add to your website to make it easy for visitors to pin your articles to one of their Boards. They just click the Pin It Button, and the article is pinned for them to view later.

Utilizing Keywords on Pinterest

Keyword phrases make the world go round, and that extends to Pinterest. You should take the time to locate the best keyword phrases so you can utilize them in multiple places, including your profile, boards, and pins.

As with all keywords, you want to choose words your target audience will use when searching for the products and services you have. And you can do this right inside Pinterest.

Do this before you start creating boards so you can make your content easy to find.

Just like SEO with Google, you want to get as specific as possible with your keywords. Keyword phrases are actually much better than single words, just like on Google.

First, go to the Search box on Pinterest and start typing in a keyword. Pinterest will auto populate to show you which keyword phrases that begin with those first words are most popular. You can choose these keywords to add to various locations to make your content super searchable.

There are several places you'll want to add your keywords to get the best optimization.

Here are places you'll want to include these keywords: On your profile

• Immediately after your business name, so people can quickly see what you do and what you can do for them.

• In your bio. A common template for including keywords in your bio is simply:

"I help_____to_____by_____

more/Click here/Sign up for my free thing: [your URL]."

On your boards

• In the name of your board - Don't use cutesy phrases to name your boards. Those won't be used for searching. Remember, the whole purpose of using Pinterest to market your business is to be introduced to new potential fans and customers.

- In the description of your board - Don't leave these blank. Many business owners do, but this is prime real estate! You can either list out your keywords in the description or write them up in a paragraph[*]. Either way, use this space! Pinterest gives you 500 characters, so you should have plenty of space.

On your pins

- You now only have 50 characters to provide a description on pins, so you will need to think carefully about how to create an inviting description that also includes keywords. Some business Pinners list several of their keywords in the description area instead of a description. You might try both and see which has the most impact.

On your pin images

- Doing this can give you a definite competitive edge. If many businesses don't even fill out their board descriptions, how many of them do you think add keywords to their images? That's right. Not many. Adding keywords to your pin images gives them an extra push up on the search ranking with Pinterest

---

[*] Right now there is no penalty for "keyword stuffing" your descriptions, though this could change in the future. For this reason, it may be best to write up a cohesive paragraph that includes your keywords rather than listing them.

and on search engines. To do this, simply change the name of the image to include meaningful keywords that someone might search for.

On your blog posts

- Include the same keywords in your blog post title and body you used in the Pinterest pin and pin images. This actually boosts the results rankings within Pinterest, as well as on search engines! Many business owners don't know that. They sometimes use conflicting keywords in their blog post and pins. Keeping them the same gives your pins a bump up in ratings, so they will be seen more often by a wider audience.

Set up your boards

Now that you know how to optimize your boards (and the rest of your account), it's time to set up your boards. Many Pinterest marketing gurus recommend setting up on 10 in the beginning and then adding to them as you go. This will provide your followers with a richer experience than if you add 25 boards, most of which are empty or practically empty. It also keeps you from being overwhelmed at the thought of filling those boards all up.

Create your boards using both broad and narrower topics. This will offer the most comprehensive profile that will continue to bring followers back to your profile. Remember to use those keywords as the board names and to include them in your board descriptions so people can easily find you.

Let's Start Pinning

It's a good idea to put up at least five pins on each board you create so that the thumbnail images won't be blank on any boards.

But what should you pin? Try these:

- Put up your evergreen blog posts
- Search for a keyword within Pinterest and look through pins until you find some you want to share with your tribe. Repin them.
- Add inspirational quotes to images
- Put short tips on images
- Search your favorite blogs and pin their content
- Use the Pinterest bookmarklet extension and pin things of interest when you come across them every day.

As with all social media, it's important that you stay consistent with your pinning. Research shows that those brands with the best followings and most engagement pin in different boards between 5-30 times per day.

That means it would be wise to use a Pinterest scheduling tool to keep up with that.

There are several of these tools. Here are the top four you may want to consider. Of course, it may be easiest to use the program you already use, if it offers Pinterest scheduling.

Popular Pinterest Scheduling Tools

Tailwind - Offers easy solutions for scheduling pins, as well as detailed analytics. It even allows you to pin the same content across multiple boards, which can come in handy. And since it integrates with Instagram and Canva, the popular low-cost image creator, you can easily pin from those two accounts, as well as directly from your computer. The also offer a free extension so you can pin content on the fly or while you surf the web.

ViralTag - This is another popular option. It's less of a scheduling tool, however than a visual marketing tool. You can use it for other social media outlets also, but you can only use it for visual images - not text, which is limiting. It's easy to use since you can drag and drop images into it. You can also upload from Dropbox, your computer, and Flickr, as well as upload them from your Instagram and Facebook profiles. They do include analytics, though they aren't as comprehensive as Tailwind.

ViralTag is a great tool for Pinterest, though you will find you also need a more general scheduling tool like Hootsuite or Buffer as well.

Hootsuite - This program now integrates with Tailwind, so while it doesn't have a standalone schedule capability itself, it's easy to include Tailwind to your profile and use it side by side with the other tools. Of course, many people love Hootsuite because of its streams feature, which keeps everything organized. You can access your Tailwind analytics from Hootsuite also, which means less flipping back and forth. Hootsuite now also offers recommendations and drafting features which people love.

Buffer - This platform has a clean interface that makes scheduling across most social media platforms a breeze. Buffer was one of the first content scheduling tools to arrive on the scene, and many people love Buffer so much, they are willing to overlook some of its limited functionality with Pinterest in particular. For example, you can only pin content to one board, not several. And they limit the size of images to 600X900 pixels only from the direct source or using their extension. While there is a way to schedule larger images, it's more time consuming if you do a lot of pinning of infographics, etc.

Exploiting the Smart Feed Algorithm

In 2014, Pinterest unveiled their Smart Feed Algorithm that uses Pinner's recent searches to show them other pins they might be interested in. If you've ever used Amazon (and who hasn't), you're used to seeing other suggestions like, "Other people who bought this also bought that." It's similar on Pinterest, and it's one of the reasons for your content staying evergreen for months and even years after you pin it.

The most important things for you as a marketer to do to get the most out of the Smart Feed is to:

• **Use only quality images** - nothing blurry or with a lot of text that's hard to read.

• **Utilize the best keywords for the board, pin, description, etc. -**

Follow the advice above for locating the best keyword phrases to include on your pins.

- **Write seductive pin descriptions that include your best keyword phrases** - make your descriptions stand out so that they get repinned more often.

- **Pin consistently** - this is important to your followers, but also to Smart Feed. Those businesses who always pin quality pins get the most attention from the algorithm.

- **Supply only helpful, relevant content** - make sure you're pinning the correct content to the correct boards to avoid confusion by the algorithm and your followers.

- **Make sure the pin image matches the content** - don't be sneaky and use pin images that don't relate to your content. Both the algorithm and your followers will catch on, and you'll lose both.

- **Repin only quality content** - always double-check the links that go back to the original content before you repin something. Spammers are everywhere, including on Pinterest. Repinning low-quality content will hurt your community reputation, your brand, and your bank account.

- **Optimize your website for Pinterest** - Add Pin It button and widgets to your blog so visitors can easily pin your content to their boards. The more often this occurs, the higher the Smart Feed recommendations will be. Make sure all your images are pinnable and use Rich Pins on your site.

Using Promoted Pins

Promoted Pins are an ad option you can use on Pinterest. But they are much more effective than placing random ads. They are very targeted and show up only to those Pinners who are looking for your content.

Promoted Pins use the power of the Smart Feed search to reach your target audience - ones who've never had a chance to meet you before.

You can use Promoted Pins for brand recognition campaigns, but there are other goals you might also use them for. You might choose to use them to boost your traffic, build your brand drive online actions (call-top-action), increase in-store sales or grow your visibility. Promoted Pins are available to all businesses and work well no matter what your niche or industry.

What's more, Promoted Pins work on the CPC (cost per click) method, so you only pay for those who actually click on your pin. But many other Pinners will also get the chance to see your brand, which will prime them for future purchasing.

It's typical for Pinners to search for something they are preparing to purchase. There is an average of 175 billion people who visit Pinterest each month, and they know that approximately 75% of the pins they will see will be from brands. Rather than distracting or interrupting a Pinner's focus like some other types of ads, Promoted Pins only show up when the Pinner has searched for that exact content. That's ideal for both you and the Pinner - you know you are getting in front of motivated people looking for your products or services and they are offered some of the best goods and services available, right from their initial search.

Additionally, when a Pinner saves your Promoted Pin to one of their boards, their followers also see it in their feeds! This little feature gives you more bang for your marketing buck, especially since pins can be found for years to come! You may end up making sales from a Promoted Pin long after you ran the ad! In fact, according to Pinterest, "Advertisers received an average of 20% more (free) clicks in the month after launching a Promoted Pin campaign."

Because Promoted Pins are keyword-based, it's vital that you optimize your campaign with the right keywords so as to get your pin in front of your targeted audience. Pinterest gives you 150 keywords for each Promoted Pin so you can include an assortment of competitive keywords that will make your marketing highly successful.

Pinterest has made it easy to set up Promoted Pin campaigns. You just chose the best pin for the goal, set your goals, determine your audience and set your CPC budget. For all the details on creating your own campaign, *go here.*

Pinterest Marketing Strategy

We've given you a lot of information so far, and you may feel like your head is spinning. But let's take a look at how simple a Pinterest marketing strategy can be. You'll notice some of the typical recommendations used in marketing efforts across the board. But you'll also see some that are specific to Pinterest.

1. Schedule pins - Earlier we mentioned a few popular social media scheduling tools that are popular with Pinterest business users. We suggest trying out a few, with their free trials, to see which one works best for you. Then, set it up and schedule away.

2. Weekly pin focus - There's no wrong day to pin, but several studies have been conducted to find out what days are most popular for which topics. Interesting, huh? We think so. Using this guide, you can make the most of your pins by focusing on the types of pins that are popular each day. Here's the breakdown according to Pinterest.

Monday - Starting off a new week of good intentions makes fitness and health the most popular.

Tuesday - Technology and gadgets rule the day.

Wednesday - We all need inspiration around Hump Day, which is why inspirational quotes are trending then.

Thursday - Everyone's getting ready for the weekend, so fashion is on everyone's mind.

Friday - Getting through that last day of the work week can be tough, which must be why comedy, especially GIFs, are popular.

Saturday - Dreams of getting away make vacation and travel the top pins.

Sunday - Ah, the day of rest leads to searching for good food and craft ideas.

Another study showed that the absolute best day for pinning is Saturday since that's a day most people can begin to rest and relax.

3. Pin Performance Measurement - The strategic marketer knows they need to track and measure their efforts to see what's paying off. Pinterest gives you analytics, as we mentioned earlier. You'll also want to pay attention to the different analytics found in the various scheduling tools. That might be one way you decide between them. Marketing can only do so much for your business if it's not been measured for success.

4. Pin Posting Frequency - Remember, the Pinners who see the most success pin anywhere from 5 to 25 times a day, throughout the day.

It's impossible to keep up with that unless you are using a smart scheduling tool. If you have time, go ahead and schedule more pins that that. You don't have to worry about overloading your follower's feeds because this social media system works differently than the rest.

5. Manage Social Media - Though some people do use different scheduling tools for various social media, it makes life in general easier if you can find one system to rule them all. Both Buffer and Hootsuite offer you the chance to schedule most social media platforms from their dashboard. Scheduling from one place just makes managing all your accounts much less time-consuming.

6. Pin on the Fly - While it's wise to schedule out your social media, it's also a good idea to pin on the fly. Pinterest has an extension to make it easy to do that, as does Hootsuite and Buffer. These extensions also let you pin any graphic you find online. When you come across something cool you want to share with your followers, you come from a place of authenticity that they'll appreciate.

7. Timing Pins - Just like there's no bad day to pin, there's no bad time to pin. But after some in-depth research, it's been determined that the following times are the best for certain topics.

Mondays at 10 pm ET - Electronics and tech

Friday at 12 pm ET - Automotive

Fridays at 3 pm ET - Fashion

Any day between 8 pm ET and midnight - Recipes that include chocolate

Any day at 8 am - Best time for food brands to get the most repins

Any day between 10-11 pm - Best time for food brands to get the most traffic.

8. Pin Consistently - by setting up and using your preferred social media scheduling tool, pinning consistently becomes easily automated. We know it's important to be consistent in all areas of business, and Pinterest marketing is no different. When you pin consistently, you'll be rewarded by both your followers and the Smart Feed Algorithm.

PINTEREST MARKETING TIPS AND TECHNIQUES

- **Collaborate on Guest Boards** - Search for guest boards where you can collaborate and share your content. Do your research, so you only join quality boards that are active and positive.

- **Create Guest Boards** - Want to connect with big influencers in your niche? Create a Guest Board (or two) and invite them to share. This is a natural way to make new connections with people who can help you grow your business. And, they will bring their followers with them.

- **Tag Influencers** - As in the case of other social media, it's important to share other people's content more than your own. This is definitely the case on Pinterest. When you share someone else's content, consider tagging them, so they know you are spreading their great stuff to your followers. Make sure you aren't doing this constantly because it will come off as spam. But do it strategically to get their attention. If they take notice and start repinning your content, your following could grow by leaps and bounds overnight.

- **Show Product Uses** - Most businesses pin images of their products, when in fact, it's more advantageous to show the product being used. This helps Pinners imagine themselves using your product. The best way to do this is to show multiple ways to use the product on one pin. Pinners will see how versatile your product is, which means they'll be less likely to live without it.

- **Use Both Wide and Narrow Keywords** - You'll want to do this with regular pins too, but it's especially important when you create a Promoted Pin. In a regular pin, you'll include both wide and narrow keywords into the description. In Promoted Pins, you get to include up to 150 keywords that are hidden from view. But make no mistake, they work in the background, making it easy for people searching to find your content.

- **Change Up your Promoted Pins Often** - Even when a campaign is really rocking, it's eventually going to stop being effective. To keep it fresh and more attractive to a wider audience, change things up on your Promoted Pins every few weeks. You can modify the image, description and even the keywords while keeping the ad running. Likewise, if a campaign isn't working well, try changing up those same features to see how it improves. You'll learn valuable lessons by tracking this. A/B testing at its easiest.

- **Use Google Analytics** - Every marketer knows the importance of using Google Analytics, and it is even useful when your marketing extends to Pinterest. Although Pinterest Analytics tracks Promoted Pin conversion, Google Analytics allows you to track the traffic that both regular and Promoted Pins send to your site. By using GA, you'll be able to see how many visitors you get from Pinterest each month and where they go on your site once they get there. This is invaluable information to have to improve the functionality of your site for visitors.

- **Be Guided by Your Followers** - Pinterest makes it easy to view your follower's profiles, which means you can see what their interests are and what they are pinning a lot of right now. This knowledge can guide you to know what you should be pinning too. By keeping an eye on what your followers are following and pinning, you'll be able to ensure you keep them fully engaged with your brand.

- **Fill in Board and Pin Descriptions** - Since we've spoken so much about optimizing your Pinterest profile, you should have gotten the idea by now, but it's worth mentioning again. The description areas are prime real estate that will make your marketing efforts so much more effective!

- **Use Hashtags Sparingly** - While hashtags can be used on Pinterest, they don't work the same way as they do on other social media platforms. The reason is that Pinterest is made to be searchable, so hashtags aren't needed in the same way - only keywords. If you chose to use hashtags, use them sparingly. Using a bunch of them at the end of your pin description is not only a waste of space you could be using wiser, but it also turns some Pinners off.

- **Add your Logo** - You should always include your logo and site URL on all Pinterest images. The goal is to get your pins repinned many times to reach more people with your brand. Since pins are so evergreen, you could lose a potential buyer or fan if they can't find where the content comes from months or years after you post it. Adding that info on the image ensures they know where to go for more fab content or details about the product.

- **Use the Right Images** - Images without faces in them get repinned 23% more than ones with faces. Enough said.

- **Don't Assume** - Don't think businesses and brands in your niche or industry are on Pinterest? You'd be surprised! Many companies believe the misconception that only DIYers and crafters are on Pinterest. Hope over there and do a little searching. You'll soon realize how vital Pinterest could be to your brand marketing.

- **Rotate your Board Focus** - When brands first go onto Pinterest to check it out, they may feel overwhelmed. *I need how many boards?!* Just remember that you don't need to pin to every single board every day. Focus on pinning and repinning on 2 or 3 boards per day and then rotate through them. That way your followers will still be getting fresh content, and you won't be overwhelmed.

- **Create step-by-step tutorial images** - Pinners love how-to tutorials! You can use these as a way to demonstrate how to use your products as an easy way to get Pinner's attention and hard earned cash. Once they learn how your products work and can imagine themselves using them, you'll quickly turn a visitor into a buyer.

CONCLUSION

If you are looking to grow your brand recognition, increase authority, break into new audiences, increase site traffic or raise your revenue, you should add Pinterest to your marketing efforts. And what business isn't doing at least one of these things all the time?

These takeaways are important to keep in mind as you begin your Pinterest marketing:

1. Even if you already have a personal account, get a business one. You miss out on all types of opportunities if you don't! You won't be able to access analytics or use Rich Pins or Promoted Pins if you only have a personal account.

2. Use keywords to make it easy for Pinners to find you in a search. Use the search box on Pinterest to find the best long-tailed keywords to use.

3. Once you have your business account set up use the unique tools Pinterest offers, such as Group Boards, Rich Pins,

and Promoted Pins. These will grow your influence in significant ways.

4. Set up your account the right way from the start. Take the time to fill in all the profile, including the keywords you found. Don't miss out by ignoring descriptions for your boards, for example.

5. Try a few Pinterest scheduling tools to see which one works best for your needs. Most of them offer a free trial, which makes it easy to try several.

6. Be consistent in your pinning. Using a scheduling tool like one of the ones we recommend is the easiest way to ensure your followers don't forget you.

7. Don't be fooled - it's not only middle-aged women who use Pinterest. And neither is it true that only DIYers and crafters use it.

Most brands can find a following that will improve their business on Pinterest.

8. Unlike any other social media platform, Pinners come to shop on Pinterest. Many purchasing decisions are made using this platform, and you too can take advantage of that.

9. Use the advice given here to ensure you are utilizing Pinterest's Smart Feed Algorithm.

10. Pinterest is only surpassed by Facebook for referral website traffic. Make use of this by providing your followers the best experience once they click onto your site. Use strong CTA's (call-to-actions) to guide them where you want them to go next.

Printed by Libri Plureos GmbH in Hamburg,
Germany